# KETO FOR CANCER

## 60+ Ketogenic Diet Recipes and Metabolic Nutrition Cookbook, just to Beat Cancer, Plus 15 Days' Meal Plan

### Dr. Natalie HealthFuel

## Reader Feedback and Inquiries

Dear Readers,

Your thoughts, questions, and feedback are invaluable to us. We invite you to share your experiences, ask questions, or provide suggestions regarding our health books and cookbooks. Your input helps us continually improve and tailor our content to better serve your needs.

Feel free to reach out to us at Chapterversecrew@gmail.com. We look forward to hearing from you and appreciate your contribution to our community of wellness enthusiasts.

Happy reading and cooking!

# Table of Content

# Introduction

In the face of adversity, we often seek unconventional paths to recovery. This cookbook, "Keto for Cancer: 60+ Ketogenic Diet Recipes and Metabolic Nutrition Cookbook," is a guide born from the amalgamation of cutting-edge nutritional science and the indomitable spirit to conquer cancer. Within these pages, we embark on a journey beyond conventional treatments, exploring the transformative potential of the ketogenic diet in the fight against cancer.

Meet Olivia, a courageous soul whose story is interwoven throughout these pages. Olivia's battle with cancer is not just a narrative; it's an inspiration that fuels the purpose of this cookbook. In the darkest moments of her struggle, Olivia discovered the profound impact of embracing a ketogenic lifestyle. Her journey serves as a beacon of hope, illustrating the resilience of the human spirit and the healing power found within the choices we make about what we consume.

This cookbook is not merely a compilation of recipes; it is a testament to the belief that nutrition can be a formidable ally in the fight against cancer. Backed by scientific insights, each recipe is crafted to support metabolic health, promote ketosis, and enhance overall well-being. We present not only a collection of delicious and satisfying dishes but a strategic approach to utilizing food as medicine.

The heart of this cookbook lies in its 15-day ketogenic meal plan, meticulously designed to simplify the transition into a metabolic state that may prove hostile to cancer cells. This plan is a practical tool, offering a structured and diverse menu to help individuals navigate the initial phases of the ketogenic journey. Whether you are a cancer patient, survivor, or a supporter in the fight against this formidable adversary, these recipes and meal plans are crafted with your holistic well-being in mind.

As we delve into the recipes and nutritional insights, let Olivia's story serve as a constant reminder that resilience and hope can be found in unexpected places. May this cookbook be a source of empowerment, guiding you towards not just a diet but a lifestyle that embraces the healing potential within every meal. Together, let us explore the realm of metabolic nutrition and forge a path towards beating cancer with the strength derived from the choices we make at our dining tables.

With determination and a fork in hand, let us embark on a journey towards renewed vitality, armed with the knowledge that every bite brings us closer to triumph over adversity.

# Understanding the Ketogenic Diet for Cancer

The ketogenic diet, initially developed to manage epilepsy, has garnered attention for its potential in cancer therapy. At its core, the ketogenic diet is characterized by a significant reduction in carbohydrates, replaced by a higher intake of healthy fats and moderate protein. This shift prompts the body to enter a metabolic state known as ketosis. For cancer patients, this dietary approach is not just about weight management; it represents a potential paradigm shift in the way we perceive and address the complexities of cancer.

## How Ketosis Affects Cancer Cells

The impact of ketosis on cancer cells is rooted in the fundamental differences between the energy metabolism of normal cells and cancer cells. Unlike healthy cells that primarily rely on glucose for energy, cancer cells often exhibit heightened glucose consumption. The ketogenic diet, by restricting glucose availability, seeks to create an environment inhospitable to these malignant cells.

In ketosis, the body produces ketones as an alternative energy source, derived from the breakdown of fats. Remarkably, while healthy cells efficiently adapt to utilizing ketones, many cancer cells struggle to thrive in this metabolic environment. This metabolic inflexibility becomes a potential Achilles' heel for cancer cells, as the ketogenic state aims to selectively starve them of their preferred energy source.

Beyond mere caloric restriction, ketosis is believed to trigger a cascade of metabolic and cellular changes that can compromise the survival mechanisms of cancer cells. This multifaceted approach underscores the ketogenic diet's potential as an adjunctive therapy, working in tandem with conventional treatments to enhance their efficacy.

## The Role of Metabolic Nutrition in Cancer Treatment

Metabolic nutrition represents a holistic approach to nourishing the body with a focus on influencing the biochemical processes that govern health. In the context of cancer treatment, metabolic nutrition acknowledges that what we eat plays a pivotal role in shaping the internal environment where cancer either flourishes or falters.

Through strategic dietary choices, metabolic nutrition seeks to optimize factors such as inflammation, insulin sensitivity, and oxidative stress—key players in the cancer microenvironment. By promoting an anti-inflammatory and metabolically supportive milieu, the goal is to create conditions that complement and augment conventional cancer therapies.

This nuanced approach recognizes the symbiotic relationship between nutrition and the body's inherent ability to defend itself. As we delve into the intricacies of metabolic nutrition, we uncover a compelling narrative—one that empowers individuals in their fight against cancer by leveraging the healing potential found within the foods they consume. This understanding forms the backbone of our exploration into the ketogenic diet's role in metabolic nutrition, as we strive to unravel the mysteries of its impact on cancer treatment and overall well-being.

# Chapter 1: Getting Started with the Ketogenic Diet

Embarking on the ketogenic journey marks a transformative step toward reshaping the body's metabolic landscape. In this chapter, we lay the foundation for your exploration of the ketogenic diet—a dietary approach with profound implications for cancer patients.

## What is the Ketogenic Diet?

The ketogenic diet, often referred to as keto, is a low-carbohydrate, high-fat, and moderate-protein dietary regimen. Its primary goal is to induce a state of ketosis, wherein the body shifts from relying on glucose as its primary energy source to burning fats and producing ketones. These ketones serve as an alternative fuel for the body and the brain. By drastically reducing carbohydrate intake, the ketogenic diet aims to alter the metabolic dynamics, offering a unique avenue for health optimization.

## Benefits of the Ketogenic Diet for Cancer Patients

For cancer patients, the ketogenic diet extends beyond conventional dietary paradigms. Research suggests that this metabolic shift may hold therapeutic potential by creating an environment less conducive to cancer cell proliferation. Beyond its potential direct impact on cancer cells, the ketogenic diet is embraced for its anti-inflammatory properties, potential improvement of insulin sensitivity, and support for overall metabolic health. This chapter explores how these benefits intersect with the unique challenges faced by cancer patients, offering a holistic approach to well-being.

## How to Achieve Ketosis

Entering into a state of ketosis requires a deliberate and mindful approach to dietary choices. This section provides practical guidance on transitioning into ketosis. From understanding macronutrient ratios to identifying ketosis-inducing foods, we offer a roadmap for achieving and maintaining this metabolic state. Whether you're a beginner or looking to fine-tune your approach, the insights provided here serve as a valuable resource on your journey toward metabolic transformation.

## Common Misconceptions about the Ketogenic Diet

As with any transformative approach, misconceptions can cloud the understanding of the ketogenic diet. This section dispels common myths and misconceptions that might hinder your journey. From concerns about nutrient deficiencies to fears about dietary monotony, we address these issues with evidence-based insights. By clarifying these misconceptions, we aim to empower you with the knowledge needed to make informed decisions about adopting the ketogenic lifestyle.

As you delve into the chapters that follow, remember that getting started with the ketogenic diet is not just about changing what's on your plate—it's a commitment to understanding and optimizing the body's metabolic pathways. Through a comprehensive exploration of the ketogenic landscape, this chapter sets the stage for a transformative journey toward health and well-being.

# Chapter 2: Essential Ingredients and Kitchen Tools

## Building a Ketogenic Pantry

**Ketogenic food basket**

Stepping into the world of ketogenic cooking requires a well-stocked pantry filled with nutrient-rich, low-carb ingredients. Here's a guide to building a ketogenic pantry that will empower you to create delicious and satisfying meals:

- **Healthy Fats:** Stock up on a variety of healthy fats, which form the foundation of the ketogenic diet. These include:

    o Oils: Extra virgin olive oil, avocado oil, coconut oil, MCT oil

    o Nuts and Seeds: Almonds, walnuts, pecans, macadamia nuts, chia seeds, flaxseeds

- o Dairy Products: Unsalted butter, ghee, heavy cream, full-fat Greek yogurt

- **Low-Carb Protein Sources:** Choose lean protein sources to meet your daily protein requirements:

  - o Meat and Poultry: Beef, chicken, pork, lamb, fish, eggs

  - o Plant-Based Proteins: Tofu, tempeh, edamame, lentils, nuts, seeds

- **Low-Carb Vegetables:** Fill your pantry with an abundance of low-carb vegetables that provide essential nutrients and fiber:

  - o Green Vegetables: Broccoli, spinach, kale, asparagus, green beans

  - o Non-Starchy Vegetables: Bell peppers, cucumbers, zucchini, celery, mushrooms

- **Other Keto-Friendly Staples:** Keep these additional items on hand to enhance your ketogenic cooking:

  - o Bone Broth: A nutrient-rich liquid that can be used in soups, stews, and sauces

- o Keto-Friendly Sweeteners: Erythritol, stevia, monk fruit

- o Spices and Herbs: A variety of spices and herbs to add flavor to your dishes without adding carbs

## Must-Have Kitchen Tools for Keto Cooking

**kitchen tools for keto cooking**

The right kitchen tools can make ketogenic cooking a breeze. Here are some essential items to consider:

- Sharp Knives: A good set of sharp knives is crucial for chopping, slicing, and dicing vegetables, proteins, and other ingredients.

- Cutting Boards: Choose durable cutting boards that won't dull your knives and are easy to clean.

- Measuring Cups and Spoons: Accurate measurements are essential for following keto recipes and ensuring the correct nutritional balance.

- Mixing Bowls: A variety of mixing bowls in different sizes will come in handy for preparing ingredients, marinades, and sauces.

- Baking Sheets and Parchment Paper: Bake low-carb treats and savory dishes with ease using baking sheets lined with parchment paper.

- Food Storage Containers: Keep your keto-friendly ingredients and meals fresh with airtight food storage containers.

- Blender or Food Processor: Blend smoothies, sauces, and purees with ease using a blender or food processor.

- Immersion Blender: Create velvety soups and sauces without the need for a traditional blender.

- Spiralizer: Turn vegetables into noodles and create low-carb pasta alternatives.

- Instant Pot: This versatile appliance can cook a variety of keto-friendly dishes, from soups and stews to beans and rice.

# Selecting Quality Ingredients for Maximum Health Benefits

When selecting ingredients for your ketogenic pantry, prioritize quality over quantity. Choose whole, unprocessed foods whenever possible. Here are some tips for selecting high-quality ingredients:

- Meat and Poultry: Opt for organic, grass-fed meat whenever possible. Look for labels that indicate the animals were raised without antibiotics or hormones.

- Dairy Products: Choose full-fat dairy products, as they contain more nutrients and healthy fats. Look for labels that indicate the cows were pasture-raised.

- Seafood: Choose wild-caught seafood over farmed varieties, as it is typically lower in contaminants and higher in nutrients.

- Vegetables: Buy local, seasonal vegetables whenever possible. Choose organic produce when available, as it may contain fewer pesticides.

- Other Ingredients: Opt for natural, unprocessed alternatives to processed foods and artificial ingredients.

By making informed choices and prioritizing quality ingredients, you can maximize the health benefits of your ketogenic diet and nourish your body with wholesome, nutritious foods.

# Chapter 3: 15-Day Ketogenic Meal Plan

Embarking on a 15-day ketogenic meal plan is a transformative step towards embracing the principles of low-carbohydrate, high-fat nutrition. This carefully crafted meal plan aims to guide you through diverse and delicious keto-friendly meals, ensuring a balanced approach to achieving and maintaining ketosis. Each day includes breakfast, lunch, dinner, and a satisfying snack.

**Day 1:**

- *Breakfast:* Avocado and Bacon Egg Cups

- *Lunch:* Grilled Chicken Caesar Salad

- *Dinner:* Zucchini Noodles with Pesto and Cherry Tomatoes

- *Snack:* Handful of Almonds

**Day 2:**

- *Breakfast:* Keto Chia Seed Pudding with Coconut Milk

- *Lunch:* Turkey and Avocado Lettuce Wraps

- *Dinner:* Baked Salmon with Lemon-Dill Butter Sauce

- *Snack:* Cheese and Veggie Sticks

**Day 3:**

- *Breakfast:* Spinach and Feta Omelette

- *Lunch:* Cobb Salad with Ranch Dressing

- *Dinner:* Beef and Broccoli Stir-Fry

- *Snack:* Keto Guacamole with Pork Rinds

**Day 4:**

- *Breakfast:* Coconut Flour Pancakes with Berries

- *Lunch:* Caprese Salad with Balsamic Glaze

- *Dinner:* Eggplant Lasagna with Ground Turkey

- *Snack:* Hard-Boiled Eggs

**Day 5:**

- *Breakfast:* Keto Green Smoothie with Spinach and Avocado

- *Lunch:* Tuna Salad Lettuce Wraps

- *Dinner:* Chicken Alfredo with Zucchini Noodles

- *Snack:* Cucumber Slices with Cream Cheese

**Day 6:**

- *Breakfast:* Bacon and Mushroom Frittata

- *Lunch:* Greek Salad with Grilled Chicken

- *Dinner:* Pork Chops with Garlic Butter

- *Snack:* Keto Fat Bombs with Dark Chocolate

**Day 7:**

- *Breakfast:* Almond Butter Keto Smoothie

- *Lunch:* Shrimp and Avocado Salad

- *Dinner:* Cauliflower Fried Rice with Shredded Chicken

- *Snack:* Pepperoni Slices with Cheese

**Day 8:**

- *Breakfast:* Keto Breakfast Burrito with Sausage and Eggs

- *Lunch:* Caesar Egg Salad Wraps

- *Dinner:* Grilled Steak with Asparagus

- *Snack:* Celery Sticks with Creamy Peanut Butter

**Day 9:**

- *Breakfast:* Keto Blueberry Muffins

- *Lunch:* Waldorf Chicken Salad

- *Dinner:* Lemon Garlic Butter Shrimp with Broccoli

- *Snack:* Keto Cheese Crisps

**Day 10:**

- *Breakfast:* Avocado and Smoked Salmon Bagels (Keto Version)

- *Lunch:* BLT Salad with Avocado

- *Dinner:* Turkey and Vegetable Skewers with Tzatziki Sauce

- *Snack:* Mixed Berries with Whipped Cream

**Day 11:**

- *Breakfast:* Keto Pumpkin Spice Latte

- *Lunch:* Egg Salad Cucumber Boats

- *Dinner:* Spaghetti Squash with Meatballs and Marinara Sauce

- *Snack:* Avocado Chocolate Mousse

**Day 12:**

- *Breakfast:* Keto Sausage and Egg Breakfast Casserole

- *Lunch:* Thai Chicken Salad with Peanut Dressing

- *Dinner:* Garlic Butter Salmon with Asparagus

- *Snack:* Seaweed Snacks

**Day 13:**

- *Breakfast:* Keto Banana Nut Muffins

- *Lunch:* Spinach and Bacon Stuffed Chicken Breast

- *Dinner:* Beef and Vegetable Kebabs

- *Snack:* Sugar-Free Jello with Whipped Cream

**Day 14:**

- *Breakfast:* Keto Chocolate Protein Smoothie

- *Lunch:* Cobb Egg Salad

- *Dinner:* Creamy Tuscan Chicken with Spinach

- *Snack:* Cheese and Pepperoni Roll-Ups

**Day 15:**

- *Breakfast:* Keto Cinnamon Roll Chia Seed Pudding

- *Lunch:* Avocado Tuna Melt Lettuce Wraps

- *Dinner:* Grilled Lamb Chops with Rosemary

- *Snack:* Greek Yogurt with Berries

Feel free to adjust portion sizes and ingredients based on your preferences and dietary requirements. This 15-day meal plan serves as a starting point on your ketogenic journey, providing a variety of flavors and textures to keep your culinary experience exciting and satisfying.

# Chapter 4: Breakfast Recipes

## 1. Keto Avocado and Bacon Egg Cups

**Ingredients:**

- 2 avocados, halved and pitted

- 4 eggs

- 4 slices of bacon, cooked and crumbled

- Salt and pepper to taste

- Fresh chives for garnish

**Nutrition:**

- Calories: 300

- Fat: 25g

- Protein: 12g

- Net Carbs: 4g

**Instructions:**

1. Preheat the oven to 375°F (190°C).

2. Scoop out a small portion of avocado flesh to make room for the egg.

3. Place avocados in a baking dish.

4. Crack one egg into each avocado half.

5. Sprinkle with bacon, salt, and pepper.

6. Bake for 12-15 minutes or until eggs are cooked to your liking.

7. Garnish with chives and serve.

## 2. Zucchini and Cheese Frittata

**Ingredients:**

- 1 cup shredded zucchini

- 4 large eggs

- 1/2 cup shredded cheddar cheese

- 2 tablespoons heavy cream

- Salt and pepper to taste

- Fresh parsley for garnish

**Nutrition:**

- Calories: 250

- Fat: 18g

- Protein: 15g

- Net Carbs: 3g

**Instructions:**

1. Preheat the oven to 350°F (175°C).

2. In a bowl, whisk together eggs, heavy cream, salt, and pepper.

3. Stir in shredded zucchini and cheddar cheese.

4. Pour the mixture into a greased baking dish.

5. Bake for 20-25 minutes until the frittata is set.

6. Garnish with fresh parsley and serve.

## 3. Coconut Flour Pancakes with Berries

**Ingredients:**

- 1/4 cup coconut flour

- 4 eggs

- 1/4 cup unsweetened almond milk

- 1/2 teaspoon baking powder

- 1/2 teaspoon vanilla extract

- Mixed berries for topping

**Nutrition:**

- Calories: 220

- Fat: 14g

- Protein: 8g

- Net Carbs: 6g

**Instructions:**

1. In a bowl, whisk together eggs, almond milk, and vanilla extract.

2. Add coconut flour and baking powder, mix until smooth.

3. Heat a skillet over medium heat and ladle the batter onto the pan.

4. Cook until bubbles form, then flip and cook the other side.

5. Top with mixed berries and serve.

## 4. Bulletproof Coffee and Variations

**Ingredients:**

- 1 cup brewed coffee

- 1 tablespoon unsalted butter

- 1 tablespoon coconut oil

- Optional: Stevia or erythritol for sweetness

**Nutrition:**

- Calories: 200

- Fat: 22g

- Protein: 0g

- Net Carbs: 0g

**Instructions:**

1. Brew a cup of coffee.

2. In a blender, combine coffee, butter, and coconut oil.

3. Blend until frothy.

4. Add sweetener if desired.

5. Pour into a mug and enjoy.

## 5. Keto Blueberry Muffins

**Ingredients:**

- 1 cup almond flour

- 1/4 cup coconut flour

- 1/4 cup melted butter

- 3 eggs

- 1/4 cup unsweetened almond milk

- 1/4 cup fresh or frozen blueberries

**Nutrition:**

- Calories: 180

- Fat: 15g

- Protein: 6g

- Net Carbs: 3g

**Instructions:**

1. Preheat the oven to 350°F (175°C).

2. In a bowl, mix almond flour, coconut flour, melted butter, eggs, and almond milk.

3. Gently fold in blueberries.

4. Spoon the batter into muffin cups.

5. Bake for 20-25 minutes or until golden brown.

# 6. Keto Green Smoothie with Spinach and Avocado

**Ingredients:**

- 1 cup unsweetened almond milk

- 1 cup fresh spinach

- 1/2 avocado

- 1/2 cucumber, peeled

- 1 tablespoon chia seeds

- Ice cubes

## Nutrition:

- Calories: 150

- Fat: 12g

- Protein: 4g

- Net Carbs: 3g

## Instructions:

1. In a blender, combine almond milk, spinach, avocado, cucumber, and chia seeds.

2. Blend until smooth.

3. Add ice cubes and blend again.

4. Pour into a glass and enjoy.

# 7. Almond Butter Keto Smoothie

## Ingredients:

- 1 cup unsweetened coconut milk

- 2 tablespoons almond butter

- 1 scoop vanilla protein powder

- Ice cubes

## Nutrition:

- Calories: 250

- Fat: 20g

- Protein: 15g

- Net Carbs: 4g

## Instructions:

1. In a blender, combine coconut milk, almond butter, and protein powder.

2. Blend until smooth.

3. Add ice cubes and blend again.

4. Pour into a glass and enjoy.

# 8. Keto Pumpkin Spice Latte

## Ingredients:

- 1 cup brewed coffee

- 1/4 cup unsweetened almond milk

- 2 tablespoons pumpkin puree

- 1/2 teaspoon pumpkin spice

- Optional: Stevia or erythritol for sweetness

## Nutrition:

- Calories: 30

- Fat: 2g

- Protein: 1g

- Net Carbs: 2g

## Instructions:

1. In a saucepan, heat almond milk, pumpkin puree, and pumpkin spice.

2. Brew a cup of coffee.

3. Combine coffee and the pumpkin spice mixture.

4. Add sweetener if desired.

5. Pour into a mug and enjoy.

# 9. Keto Banana Nut Muffins

## Ingredients:

- 1 cup almond flour

- 1/4 cup coconut flour

- 2 ripe bananas, mashed

- 1/4 cup melted coconut oil

- 3 eggs

- 1/2 cup chopped walnuts

**Nutrition:**

- Calories: 220

- Fat: 18g

- Protein: 6g

- Net Carbs: 4g

**Instructions:**

1. Preheat the oven to 350°F (175°C).

2. In a bowl, mix almond flour, coconut flour, mashed bananas, melted coconut oil, and eggs.

3. Fold in chopped walnuts.

4. Spoon the batter into muffin cups.

5. Bake for 20-25 minutes or until a toothpick comes out clean.

## 10. Keto Chocolate Protein Smoothie

**Ingredients:**

- 1 cup unsweetened almond milk

- 1 scoop chocolate protein powder

- 2 tablespoons unsweetened cocoa powder

- 1 tablespoon almond butter

- Ice cubes

**Nutrition:**

- Calories: 180

- Fat: 12g

- Protein: 15g

- Net Carbs: 3g

**Instructions:**

1. In a blender, combine almond milk, chocolate protein powder, cocoa powder, and almond butter.

2. Blend until smooth.

3. Add ice cubes and blend again.

4. Pour into a glass and enjoy.

These recipes provide a variety of delicious and nutritious options to kickstart your day while adhering to the principles of the ketogenic diet. Feel free to adjust ingredients and portions based on your taste preferences and dietary needs.

# Chapter 4: Lunch Recipes

In this chapter, we explore a collection of hearty and nutritionally rich lunch recipes tailored for those embracing the ketogenic lifestyle in their fight against cancer. Each recipe is designed with carefully selected ingredients to align with the principles of a low-carbohydrate, high-fat diet.

## 1. Grilled Chicken Caesar Salad

**Ingredients:**

- 2 boneless, skinless chicken breasts

- Romaine lettuce

- Parmesan cheese, grated

- Cherry tomatoes, halved

- Caesar dressing (keto-friendly)

- Olive oil

- Salt and pepper to taste

**Instructions:**

1. Season chicken breasts with salt and pepper, then grill until fully cooked.

2. Slice grilled chicken into strips.

3. In a bowl, toss Romaine lettuce, cherry tomatoes, and Parmesan cheese.

4. Add grilled chicken strips to the salad.

5. Drizzle with keto-friendly Caesar dressing and olive oil.

6. Toss the salad until well-coated and serve.

**Nutrition (per serving):**

- Calories: 400

- Protein: 30g

- Fat: 25g

- Carbohydrates: 7g

- Fiber: 3g

## 2. Turkey and Avocado Lettuce Wraps

**Ingredients:**

- Sliced turkey breast

- Avocado, sliced

- Lettuce leaves (butter or iceberg)

- Mayonnaise (keto-friendly)

- Mustard

- Salt and pepper to taste

**Instructions:**

1. Lay out lettuce leaves and place turkey slices on each leaf.

2. Add avocado slices on top of the turkey.

3. Drizzle with keto-friendly mayonnaise and mustard.

4. Season with salt and pepper to taste.

5. Wrap the ingredients in the lettuce leaves and secure with toothpicks if needed.

6. Serve chilled.

**Nutrition (per serving):**

- Calories: 280

- Protein: 20g

- Fat: 20g

- Carbohydrates: 5g

- Fiber: 3g

# 3. Beef and Broccoli Stir-Fry

**Ingredients:**

- Thinly sliced beef sirloin

- Broccoli florets

- Soy sauce (low-sodium, keto-friendly)

- Sesame oil

- Garlic, minced

- Ginger, grated

- Salt and pepper to taste

**Instructions:**

1. In a pan, sauté minced garlic and grated ginger in sesame oil.

2. Add sliced beef and cook until browned.

3. Stir in broccoli florets and cook until tender-crisp.

4. Pour in low-sodium, keto-friendly soy sauce.

5. Season with salt and pepper to taste.

6. Serve hot.

**Nutrition (per serving):**

- Calories: 350

- Protein: 25g

- Fat: 22g

- Carbohydrates: 6g

- Fiber: 2g

## 4. Eggplant Lasagna with Ground Turkey

**Ingredients:**

- Eggplant, thinly sliced

- Ground turkey

- Keto-friendly marinara sauce

- Mozzarella cheese, shredded

- Ricotta cheese

- Parmesan cheese, grated

- Italian seasoning

- Salt and pepper to taste

**Instructions:**

1. Sauté ground turkey until browned, season with Italian seasoning, salt, and pepper.

2. In a baking dish, layer sliced eggplant, ground turkey, marinara sauce, and cheeses.

3. Repeat layers, finishing with a cheese layer on top.

4. Bake until bubbly and golden.

5. Let it cool before slicing and serving.

**Nutrition (per serving):**

- Calories: 320

- Protein: 28g

- Fat: 18g

- Carbohydrates: 8g

- Fiber: 4g

# 5. Keto Avocado and Bacon Lettuce Wraps

**Ingredients:**

- Ripe avocados, sliced

- Bacon strips, cooked

- Lettuce leaves (butter or iceberg)

- Mayonnaise (keto-friendly)

- Mustard

- Salt and pepper to taste

**Instructions:**

1. Arrange lettuce leaves and place avocado slices on each leaf.

2. Add cooked bacon strips on top.

3. Drizzle with keto-friendly mayonnaise and mustard.

4. Season with salt and pepper to taste.

5. Wrap the ingredients in the lettuce leaves and serve.

**Nutrition (per serving):**

- Calories: 320

- Protein: 10g

- Fat: 28g

- Carbohydrates: 5g

- Fiber: 3g

# 6. Caprese Salad with Balsamic Glaze

**Ingredients:**

- Fresh mozzarella, sliced

- Cherry tomatoes, halved

- Fresh basil leaves

- Balsamic glaze (keto-friendly)

- Olive oil

- Salt and pepper to taste

**Instructions:**

1. Arrange mozzarella slices and cherry tomato halves on a plate.

2. Tuck fresh basil leaves between the mozzarella and tomatoes.

3. Drizzle with keto-friendly balsamic glaze and olive oil.

4. Season with salt and pepper to taste.

5. Serve chilled.

**Nutrition (per serving):**

- Calories: 250

- Protein: 12g

- Fat: 20g

- Carbohydrates: 7g

- Fiber: 2g

## 7. Cobb Salad with Ranch Dressing

**Ingredients:**

- Grilled chicken breast, diced

- Bacon, cooked and crumbled

- Avocado, diced

- Blue cheese, crumbled

- Hard-boiled eggs, sliced

- Romaine lettuce

- Keto-friendly ranch dressing

**Instructions:**

1. Arrange Romaine lettuce on a plate.

2. Add diced chicken, crumbled bacon, diced avocado, blue cheese, and sliced hard-boiled eggs.

3. Drizzle with keto-friendly ranch dressing.

4. Toss the salad gently and serve.

**Nutrition (per serving):**

- Calories: 380

- Protein: 30g

- Fat: 28g

- Carbohydrates: 8g

- Fiber: 4g

## 8. Keto Chicken Alfredo with Zucchini Noodles

**Ingredients:**

- Zucchini, spiralized into noodles

- Cooked chicken breast, shredded

- Heavy cream

- Parmesan cheese, grated

- Garlic, minced

- Butter

- Salt and pepper to taste

**Instructions:**

1. In a pan, sauté minced garlic in butter until fragrant.

2. Add shredded chicken and cook until heated through.

3. Pour in heavy cream and stir in grated Parmesan cheese.

4. Season with salt and pepper to taste.

5. Toss in spiralized zucchini noodles and cook until tender.

6. Serve hot.

**Nutrition (per serving):**

- Calories: 320

- Protein: 25g

- Fat: 22g

- Carbohydrates: 6g

- Fiber: 2g

# 9. Keto Tuna Salad Lettuce Wraps

## Ingredients:

- Canned tuna, drained

- Celery, finely chopped

- Red onion, finely chopped

- Mayonnaise (keto-friendly)

- Dijon mustard

- Lettuce leaves (butter or iceberg)

- Salt and pepper to taste

## Instructions:

1. In a bowl, mix tuna, chopped celery, chopped red onion, keto-friendly mayonnaise, and Dijon mustard.

2. Season with salt and pepper to taste.

3. Spoon the tuna mixture onto lettuce leaves.

4. Wrap the leaves around the filling and secure with toothpicks if needed.

5. Serve chilled.

**Nutrition (per serving):**

- Calories: 280

- Protein: 20g

- Fat: 18g

- Carbohydrates: 5g

- Fiber: 2g

# 10. Keto Thai Chicken Salad with Peanut Dressing

**Ingredients:**

- Grilled chicken thighs, sliced

- Mixed salad greens

- Cucumber, julienned

- Carrots, julienned

- Red bell pepper, sliced

- Keto-friendly peanut dressing

- Fresh cilantro, chopped

- Peanuts, crushed

**Instructions:**

1. Arrange mixed salad greens on a plate.

2. Top with sliced grilled chicken, julienned cucumber, julienned carrots, and sliced red bell pepper.

3. Drizzle with keto-friendly peanut dressing.

4. Sprinkle with chopped fresh cilantro and crushed peanuts.

5. Serve immediately.

**Nutrition (per serving):**

- Calories: 350

- Protein: 25g

- Fat: 22g

- Carbohydrates: 8g

- Fiber: 3g

Feel free to adapt these recipes based on your preferences and dietary needs. These lunch options not only align with the principles of the ketogenic diet but also aim to provide a burst of flavors to elevate your dining experience while supporting your health goals in the fight against cancer.

# Chapter 5: Dinner Recipes

## 1. Grilled Salmon with Lemon-Dill Butter Sauce

**Ingredients:**

- Salmon fillets

- Butter

- Fresh dill

- Lemon

- Salt and pepper to taste

**Nutritional Information (per serving):**

- Calories: 300

- Protein: 25g

- Fat: 20g

- Carbohydrates: 1g

**Instructions:**

1. Season salmon fillets with salt and pepper.

2. Grill salmon until cooked through.

3. In a saucepan, melt butter, add fresh dill, and squeeze lemon juice.

4. Pour the lemon-dill butter sauce over the grilled salmon.

## 2. Eggplant Lasagna with Ground Turkey

**Ingredients:**

- Eggplant

- Ground turkey

- Tomato sauce (sugar-free)

- Mozzarella cheese

- Ricotta cheese

- Italian seasoning

**Nutritional Information (per serving):**

- Calories: 400

- Protein: 30g

- Fat: 25g

- Carbohydrates: 10g

**Instructions:**

1. Slice eggplant into thin strips.

2. Brown ground turkey in a pan and mix with tomato sauce and Italian seasoning.

3. Layer eggplant, turkey mixture, mozzarella, and ricotta in a baking dish.

4. Bake until bubbly and golden.

# 3. Beef and Broccoli Stir-Fry

**Ingredients:**

- Beef strips

- Broccoli florets

- Coconut aminos

- Sesame oil

- Garlic and ginger

**Nutritional Information (per serving):**

- Calories: 350

- Protein: 28g

- Fat: 22g

- Carbohydrates: 8g

**Instructions:**

1. Sauté beef strips in sesame oil until browned.

2. Add minced garlic and ginger, followed by broccoli.

3. Pour in coconut aminos and stir until broccoli is tender.

# 4. Chicken Alfredo with Zucchini Noodles

## Ingredients:

- Chicken breast

- Zucchini

- Heavy cream

- Parmesan cheese

- Garlic

- Salt and pepper

## Nutritional Information (per serving):

- Calories: 320

- Protein: 27g

- Fat: 18g

- Carbohydrates: 6g

## Instructions:

1. Cook chicken in a pan until fully cooked.

2. Spiralize zucchini into noodles.

3. In the same pan, add heavy cream, Parmesan, garlic, salt, and pepper.

4. Toss zucchini noodles in the Alfredo sauce.

## 5. Cauliflower Fried Rice with Shredded Chicken

**Ingredients:**

- Cauliflower rice

- Shredded chicken

- Mixed vegetables (peas, carrots, and bell peppers)

- Eggs

- Soy sauce (low-sodium)

**Nutritional Information (per serving):**

- Calories: 280

- Protein: 24g

- Fat: 15g

- Carbohydrates: 10g

**Instructions:**

1. Sauté cauliflower rice and mixed vegetables.

2. Add shredded chicken and scramble eggs into the mix.

3. Stir in low-sodium soy sauce.

# 6. Garlic Butter Salmon with Asparagus

**Ingredients:**

- Salmon fillets

- Asparagus

- Butter

- Garlic

- Lemon

- Salt and pepper

**Nutritional Information (per serving):**

- Calories: 320

- Protein: 28g

- Fat: 20g

- Carbohydrates: 8g

**Instructions:**

1. Season salmon with salt, pepper, and minced garlic.

2. Sear salmon in butter until cooked.

3. In the same pan, cook asparagus with lemon juice.

# 7. Creamy Tuscan Chicken with Spinach

**Ingredients:**

- Chicken thighs

- Heavy cream

- Spinach

- Sun-dried tomatoes

- Parmesan cheese

- Italian seasoning

**Nutritional Information (per serving):**

- Calories: 380

- Protein: 26g

- Fat: 28g

- Carbohydrates: 5g

**Instructions:**

1. Sear chicken thighs until golden.

2. Add heavy cream, Parmesan, spinach, sun-dried tomatoes, and Italian seasoning.

3. Simmer until the sauce thickens.

# 8. Grilled Steak with Asparagus

**Ingredients:**

- Ribeye steak

- Asparagus

- Olive oil

- Garlic

- Rosemary

- Salt and pepper

**Nutritional Information (per serving):**

- Calories: 450

- Protein: 35g

- Fat: 32g

- Carbohydrates: 5g

**Instructions:**

1. Marinate steak with olive oil, minced garlic, rosemary, salt, and pepper.

2. Grill steak to desired doneness.

3. Grill asparagus until tender.

# 9. Lemon Garlic Butter Shrimp with Broccoli

**Ingredients:**

- Shrimp

- Broccoli florets

- Butter

- Garlic

- Lemon

- Parsley

**Nutritional Information (per serving):**

- Calories: 280

- Protein: 24g

- Fat: 18g

- Carbohydrates: 10g

**Instructions:**

1. Sauté shrimp in garlic and butter until pink.

2. Steam broccoli separately.

3. Combine shrimp, broccoli, and finish with lemon juice and parsley.

# 10. Pork Chops with Garlic Butter

**Ingredients:**

- Pork chops

- Butter

- Garlic

- Thyme

- Salt and pepper

**Nutritional Information (per serving):**

- Calories: 400

- Protein: 30g

- Fat: 28g

- Carbohydrates: 2g

**Instructions:**

1. Season pork chops with salt, pepper, and thyme.

2. Sear in a pan with garlic and butter until fully cooked.

3. Baste with garlic butter before serving.

Adjust portion sizes according to your dietary needs, and feel free to customize these recipes to suit your taste preferences. These dinners are not only keto-friendly but also designed to provide nourishment and support on your journey to beat cancer.

# Chapter 6: Snack Recipes

## 1. Avocado and Bacon Deviled Eggs

**Ingredients:**

- 6 hard-boiled eggs

- 1 ripe avocado

- 4 slices of crispy bacon, crumbled

- 1 tablespoon mayonnaise

- 1 teaspoon Dijon mustard

- Salt and pepper to taste

- Fresh chives for garnish

**Nutrition:**

- Calories: 120 per serving

- Fat: 9g

- Protein: 6g

- Net Carbs: 2g

**Instructions:**

1. Cut the hard-boiled eggs in half, and carefully remove the yolks.

2. Mash the yolks with avocado, mayonnaise, Dijon mustard, salt, and pepper.

3. Spoon the mixture back into the egg whites.

4. Top with crumbled bacon and garnish with fresh chives.

5. Refrigerate for 30 minutes before serving.

# 2. Parmesan Crisps

## Ingredients:

- 1 cup shredded Parmesan cheese

## Nutrition:

- Calories: 100 per serving

- Fat: 7g

- Protein: 10g

- Net Carbs: 1g

## Instructions:

1. Preheat the oven to 400°F (200°C) and line a baking sheet with parchment paper.

2. Place small heaps of Parmesan cheese on the parchment paper, leaving space between each.

3. Flatten and shape the heaps into circles.

4. Bake for 5-7 minutes or until golden and crispy.

5. Allow to cool before serving.

## 3. Keto Guacamole with Veggie Sticks

**Ingredients:**

- 3 avocados, peeled and mashed

- 1 tomato, diced

- 1/4 cup red onion, finely chopped

- 1/4 cup fresh cilantro, chopped

- 1 lime, juiced

- Salt and pepper to taste

- Assorted vegetable sticks (cucumber, bell pepper, celery) for dipping

**Nutrition:**

- Calories: 150 per serving

- Fat: 12g

- Protein: 2g

- Net Carbs: 6g

**Instructions:**

1. In a bowl, combine mashed avocados, diced tomato, red onion, cilantro, lime juice, salt, and pepper.

2. Mix well and adjust seasoning to taste.

3. Serve with assorted vegetable sticks for dipping.

## 4. Buffalo Cauliflower Bites

**Ingredients:**

- 1 medium cauliflower, cut into florets

- 1/2 cup almond flour

- 1/2 cup unsweetened almond milk

- 1 teaspoon garlic powder

- 1 teaspoon onion powder

- 1/2 cup buffalo sauce

- Ranch dressing for dipping (optional)

**Nutrition:**

- Calories: 120 per serving

- Fat: 8g

- Protein: 4g

- Net Carbs: 4g

**Instructions:**

1. Preheat the oven to 450°F (230°C) and line a baking sheet with parchment paper.

2. In a bowl, mix almond flour, almond milk, garlic powder, and onion powder to create a batter.

3. Dip each cauliflower floret into the batter, coating evenly, and place on the baking sheet.

4. Bake for 20-25 minutes or until golden brown.

5. Toss the baked cauliflower in buffalo sauce.

6. Serve with ranch dressing for dipping.

# 5. Cheese and Pepperoni Roll-Ups

**Ingredients:**

- Sliced pepperoni

- Mozzarella cheese sticks

**Nutrition:**

- Calories: 120 per serving

- Fat: 10g

- Protein: 7g

- Net Carbs: 1g

**Instructions:**

1. Place a slice of pepperoni on a flat surface.

2. Lay a mozzarella cheese stick on the pepperoni and roll it up.

3. Repeat with desired quantity.

4. Secure with toothpicks if needed.

5. Serve as is or lightly pan-fry for a warm, melty treat.

## 6. Keto Fat Bombs with Dark Chocolate

**Ingredients:**

- 1/2 cup coconut oil

- 1/4 cup almond butter

- 2 tablespoons unsweetened cocoa powder

- 1 tablespoon powdered erythritol

- 1/2 teaspoon vanilla extract

- A pinch of salt

**Nutrition:**

- Calories: 90 per serving

- Fat: 9g

- Protein: 1g

- Net Carbs: 1g

**Instructions:**

1. Melt coconut oil and almond butter in a microwave-safe bowl.

2. Stir in cocoa powder, erythritol, vanilla extract, and a pinch of salt.

3. Pour the mixture into silicone molds or an ice cube tray.

4. Freeze for 1-2 hours until solid.

5. Remove from molds and store in the freezer.

# 7. Keto Cheese Crisps

**Ingredients:**

- 1 cup shredded cheddar cheese

**Nutrition:**

- Calories: 100 per serving

- Fat: 8g

- Protein: 6g

- Net Carbs: 1g

**Instructions:**

1. Preheat the oven to 375°F (190°C) and line a baking sheet with parchment paper.

2. Place small mounds of shredded cheddar on the parchment paper, leaving space between each.

3. Flatten and shape the mounds into circles.

4. Bake for 7-10 minutes or until the edges are golden and crisp.

5. Allow to cool before serving.

## 8. Seaweed Snacks

**Ingredients:**

- Roasted seaweed sheets

**Nutrition:**

- Calories: 20 per serving

- Fat: 1g

- Protein: 1g

- Net Carbs: 0g

**Instructions:**

1. Purchase pre-packaged roasted seaweed sheets.

2. Enjoy them as a light and crunchy snack on their own or with a dip of your choice.

# 9. Keto Cheese and Bacon Dip

**Ingredients:**

- 1 cup shredded sharp cheddar cheese

- 1/2 cup cream cheese

- 1/4 cup cooked and crumbled bacon

- 2 tablespoons sour cream

- 1/2 teaspoon garlic powder

- Chopped green onions for garnish

**Nutrition:**

- Calories: 120 per serving

- Fat: 10g

- Protein: 5g

- Net Carbs: 2g

**Instructions:**

1. In a microwave-safe bowl, combine cheddar cheese, cream cheese, bacon, sour cream, and garlic powder.

2. Microwave in 30-second intervals, stirring until smooth.

3. Garnish with chopped green onions before serving.

4. Serve with vegetable sticks or keto-friendly crackers.

# 10. Keto Chocolate Avocado Mousse

**Ingredients:**

- 2 ripe avocados

- 1/4 cup unsweetened cocoa powder

- 1/4 cup powdered erythritol

- 1/4 cup almond milk

- 1 teaspoon vanilla extract

- A pinch of salt

**Nutrition:**

- Calories: 150 per serving

- Fat: 12g

- Protein: 2g

- Net Carbs: 4g

**Instructions:**

1. In a blender, combine avocados, cocoa powder, erythritol, almond milk, vanilla extract, and a pinch of salt.

2. Blend until smooth and creamy.

3. Refrigerate for at least 1 hour before serving.

4. Garnish with a dollop of whipped cream if desired.

# Chapter 4: Desserts Recipes

Indulging in delectable desserts on a ketogenic diet is not only possible but also a delightful part of your journey. Here are 10 Keto-friendly dessert recipes that not only satisfy your sweet tooth but are crafted with ingredients to support your health and well-being.

## 1. Chocolate Avocado Mousse

**Ingredients:**

- 2 ripe avocados

- 1/4 cup unsweetened cocoa powder

- 1/4 cup coconut milk

- 1/4 cup powdered erythritol

- 1 tsp vanilla extract

- Pinch of salt

**Nutrition (per serving):**

- Calories: 150

- Fat: 12g

- Net Carbs: 3g

- Protein: 2g

**Instructions:**

1. Blend avocados, cocoa powder, coconut milk, erythritol, vanilla extract, and salt until smooth.

2. Refrigerate for at least 1 hour before serving.

## 2. Berry Coconut Fat Bombs

**Ingredients:**

- 1/2 cup coconut oil

- 1/2 cup mixed berries (blueberries, raspberries, strawberries)

- 2 tbsp unsweetened shredded coconut

- 1 tbsp powdered erythritol

**Nutrition (per serving, makes 10 fat bombs):**

- Calories: 80

- Fat: 9g

- Net Carbs: 1g

- Protein: 0.5g

**Instructions:**

1. Melt coconut oil and mix with berries, shredded coconut, and erythritol.

2. Pour into molds and freeze until solid.

# 3. Almond Butter Keto Cookies

**Ingredients:**

- 1 cup almond butter

- 1/2 cup erythritol

- 1 egg

- 1 tsp vanilla extract

- 1/2 tsp baking soda

- Pinch of salt

**Nutrition (per cookie, makes 12 cookies):**

- Calories: 120

- Fat: 10g

- Net Carbs: 2g

- Protein: 4g

**Instructions:**

1. Mix almond butter, erythritol, egg, vanilla extract, baking soda, and salt.

2. Form into cookies on a baking sheet and bake at 350°F (175°C) for 10-12 minutes.

# 4. Lemon Cheesecake Bites

**Ingredients:**

- 8 oz cream cheese

- 1/4 cup powdered erythritol

- Zest and juice of 1 lemon

- 1 tsp vanilla extract

**Nutrition (per serving, makes 8 bites):**

- Calories: 120

- Fat: 11g

- Net Carbs: 2g

- Protein: 2g

**Instructions:**

1. Beat cream cheese, erythritol, lemon zest, lemon juice, and vanilla extract until smooth.

2. Spoon into bite-sized portions and refrigerate for at least 2 hours.

# 5. Chocolate Peanut Butter Fat Bombs

**Ingredients:**

- 1/2 cup coconut oil

- 1/4 cup unsweetened cocoa powder

- 1/4 cup peanut butter

- 2 tbsp powdered erythritol

**Nutrition (per serving, makes 10 fat bombs):**

- Calories: 90

- Fat: 9g

- Net Carbs: 1g

- Protein: 1.5g

**Instructions:**

1. Melt coconut oil and mix with cocoa powder, peanut butter, and erythritol.

2. Pour into molds and freeze until solid.

# 6. Vanilla Almond Panna Cotta

**Ingredients:**

- 2 cups almond milk

- 1/4 cup powdered erythritol

- 2 tsp gelatin

- 1 tsp vanilla extract

**Nutrition (per serving, makes 4 servings):**

- Calories: 60

- Fat: 5g

- Net Carbs: 1g

- Protein: 2g

**Instructions:**

1. Heat almond milk and erythritol until warm. Dissolve gelatin in the mixture.

2. Stir in vanilla extract and pour into molds. Refrigerate until set.

# 7. Keto Coconut Macaroons

**Ingredients:**

- 3 cups shredded unsweetened coconut

- 1/2 cup coconut oil

- 1/4 cup powdered erythritol

- 1 tsp vanilla extract

- Pinch of salt

**Nutrition (per macaroon, makes 12 macaroons):**

- Calories: 120

- Fat: 12g

- Net Carbs: 2g

- Protein: 1g

**Instructions:**

1. Mix shredded coconut, melted coconut oil, erythritol, vanilla extract, and salt.

2. Form into macaroons on a baking sheet and bake at 325°F (163°C) for 15-18 minutes.

# 8. Raspberry Chia Seed Pudding

**Ingredients:**

- 1/2 cup raspberries

- 2 tbsp chia seeds

- 1 cup unsweetened almond milk

- 1 tbsp powdered erythritol

- 1/2 tsp vanilla extract

**Nutrition (per serving, makes 2 servings):**

- Calories: 70

- Fat: 4g

- Net Carbs: 4g

- Protein: 2g

**Instructions:**

1. Mash raspberries and mix with chia seeds, almond milk, erythritol, and vanilla extract.

2. Refrigerate for at least 4 hours or overnight.

# 9. Keto-Friendly Dark Chocolate Bark

**Ingredients:**

- 1 cup dark chocolate (85% cocoa or higher)

- 1/4 cup chopped nuts (almonds, walnuts)

- 2 tbsp unsweetened shredded coconut

**Nutrition (per serving, makes 8 servings):**

- Calories: 100

- Fat: 8g

- Net Carbs: 2g

- Protein: 2g

**Instructions:**

1. Melt dark chocolate and spread onto a parchment paper-lined tray.

2. Sprinkle chopped nuts and shredded coconut on top. Refrigerate until set.

# 10. Pistachio Keto Ice Cream

**Ingredients:**

- 2 cups heavy cream

- 1/2 cup powdered erythritol

- 1 tsp vanilla extract

- 1/2 cup chopped pistachios

**Nutrition (per serving, makes 6 servings):**

- Calories: 250

- Fat: 25g

- Net Carbs: 2g

- Protein: 2g

**Instructions:**

1. Whip heavy cream until stiff peaks form. Mix in erythritol and vanilla extract.

2. Fold in chopped pistachios and freeze until firm.

These dessert recipes are not only delicious but also nutritionally mindful, allowing you to satisfy your sweet cravings while adhering to the principles of a ketogenic lifestyle. Enjoy these treats as part of your journey towards well-being and balance.

# Chapter 8: Beverages and Smoothies

Harnessing the power of ketogenic nutrition extends beyond solid meals to refreshing beverages and smoothies. These recipes are not only delicious but also designed to support a ketogenic lifestyle, offering a variety of flavors to tantalize your taste buds while adhering to the principles of low-carbohydrate, high-fat nutrition.

## 1. Keto Avocado Berry Smoothie

**Ingredients:**

- 1/2 avocado

- 1/2 cup mixed berries (strawberries, blueberries, raspberries)

- 1 cup unsweetened almond milk

- 1 tablespoon chia seeds

- Ice cubes

**Nutrition:**

- Calories: 250

- Net Carbs: 8g

- Fat: 20g

- Protein: 5g

**Instructions:**

1. Combine avocado, berries, almond milk, and chia seeds in a blender.

2. Blend until smooth.

3. Add ice cubes and blend again until desired consistency is reached.

4. Pour into a glass and enjoy the creamy, nutrient-packed goodness.

## 2. Keto Green Tea Latte

**Ingredients:**

- 1 cup brewed green tea

- 1/4 cup unsweetened almond milk

- 1 tablespoon coconut oil

- 1/2 teaspoon matcha powder

- Stevia or erythritol to taste

**Nutrition:**

- Calories: 40

- Net Carbs: 1g

- Fat: 4g

- Protein: 0g

**Instructions:**

1. Brew green tea and let it cool slightly.

2. In a blender, combine green tea, almond milk, coconut oil, matcha powder, and sweetener.

3. Blend until frothy.

4. Pour into a mug and savor the energizing, antioxidant-rich blend.

## 3. Keto Electrolyte Lemonade

**Ingredients:**

- 2 cups water

- Juice of 1 lemon

- 1/4 teaspoon sea salt

- 1/4 teaspoon potassium chloride (No-Salt)

- Stevia or erythritol to taste

**Nutrition:**

- Calories: 5

- Net Carbs: 1g

- Fat: 0g

- Protein: 0g

**Instructions:**

1. Mix water, lemon juice, sea salt, potassium chloride, and sweetener in a pitcher.

2. Stir until well combined.

3. Chill in the refrigerator or serve over ice for a refreshing and hydrating keto-friendly lemonade.

## 4. Keto Chocolate Almond Milkshake

**Ingredients:**

- 1 cup unsweetened almond milk

- 2 tablespoons unsweetened cocoa powder

- 1 tablespoon almond butter

- 1/2 teaspoon vanilla extract

- Ice cubes

**Nutrition:**

- Calories: 120

- Net Carbs: 3g

- Fat: 10g

- Protein: 3g

**Instructions:**

1. Blend almond milk, cocoa powder, almond butter, and vanilla extract until smooth.

2. Add ice cubes and blend again until creamy.

3. Pour into a glass and relish the rich chocolatey goodness.

# 5. Keto Coffee Smoothie

**Ingredients:**

- 1 cup brewed coffee, chilled

- 1/4 cup heavy cream

- 1 tablespoon MCT oil

- 1/2 teaspoon cinnamon

- Ice cubes

**Nutrition:**

- Calories: 180

- Net Carbs: 1g

- Fat: 18g

- Protein: 1g

**Instructions:**

1. Blend chilled coffee, heavy cream, MCT oil, and cinnamon until frothy.

2. Add ice cubes and blend again for a refreshing coffee-infused smoothie.

3. Pour into a glass and enjoy the caffeine kick.

# 6. Keto Berry Coconut Smoothie Bowl

**Ingredients:**

- 1/2 cup mixed berries (strawberries, blueberries, raspberries)

- 1/4 cup coconut milk

- 1 tablespoon chia seeds

- Unsweetened shredded coconut for topping

**Nutrition:**

- Calories: 200

- Net Carbs: 8g

- Fat: 15g

- Protein: 4g

**Instructions:**

1. Blend mixed berries, coconut milk, and chia seeds until smooth.

2. Pour into a bowl and top with shredded coconut.

3. Spoon your way through this satisfying and nutrient-packed smoothie bowl.

# 7. Keto Golden Milk Latte

**Ingredients:**

- 1 cup unsweetened almond milk

- 1 teaspoon turmeric powder

- 1/2 teaspoon cinnamon

- 1/4 teaspoon ginger powder

- Pinch of black pepper

- Stevia or erythritol to taste

**Nutrition:**

- Calories: 30

- Net Carbs: 1g

- Fat: 3g

- Protein: 1g

**Instructions:**

1. Heat almond milk in a saucepan.

2. Whisk in turmeric, cinnamon, ginger, black pepper, and sweetener.

3. Pour into a mug and relish the warm, spiced goodness of this keto-friendly golden milk.

# 8. Keto Berry Protein Smoothie

**Ingredients:**

- 1/2 cup mixed berries (strawberries, blueberries, raspberries)

- 1 scoop keto-friendly protein powder

- 1 cup unsweetened almond milk

- 1 tablespoon almond butter

- Ice cubes

**Nutrition:**

- Calories: 250

- Net Carbs: 5g

- Fat: 17g

- Protein: 20g

**Instructions:**

1. Blend mixed berries, protein powder, almond milk, and almond butter until well combined.

2. Add ice cubes and blend again for a protein-packed, fruity delight.

3. Pour into a glass and savor the satisfying blend of flavors.

# 9. Keto Minty Avocado Smoothie

**Ingredients:**

- 1/2 avocado

- 1 cup spinach

- 1/4 cup fresh mint leaves

- 1 cup unsweetened coconut milk

- Stevia or erythritol to taste

**Nutrition:**

- Calories: 180

- Net Carbs: 4g

- Fat: 16g

- Protein: 2g

**Instructions:**

1. Blend avocado, spinach, mint leaves, coconut milk, and sweetener until smooth.

2. Pour into a glass and enjoy the vibrant green goodness of this keto-friendly minty avocado smoothie.

## 10. Keto Vanilla Almond Shake

**Ingredients:**

- 1 cup unsweetened almond milk

- 1/2 teaspoon vanilla extract

- 1 tablespoon almond butter

- 1/4 teaspoon cinnamon

- Ice cubes

**Nutrition:**

- Calories: 120

- Net Carbs: 2g

- Fat: 10g

- Protein: 3g

**Instructions:**

1. Blend almond milk, vanilla extract, almond butter, and cinnamon until creamy.

2. Add ice cubes and blend again for a satisfyingly sweet and nutty keto shake.

3. Pour into a glass and relish the comforting flavors.

## 11. Keto Raspberry Lemonade Slushie

**Ingredients:**

- 1/2 cup raspberries

- Juice of 1 lemon

- 1 cup ice

- 1/4 cup water

- Stevia or erythritol to taste

**Nutrition:**

- Calories: 30

- Net Carbs: 4g

- Fat: 0g

- Protein: 1g

**Instructions:**

1. Blend raspberries, lemon juice, ice, water, and sweetener until slushie consistency is achieved.

2. Pour into a glass and enjoy the zesty refreshment of this keto-friendly slushie.

## 12. Keto Coconut Matcha Smoothie

**Ingredients:**

- 1 cup unsweetened coconut milk

- 1 teaspoon matcha powder

- 1/2 tablespoon MCT oil

- Stevia or erythritol to taste

**Nutrition:**

- Calories: 80

- Net Carbs: 1g

- Fat: 7g

- Protein: 1g

**Instructions:**

1. Blend coconut milk, matcha powder, MCT oil, and sweetener until smooth.

2. Pour into a glass and relish the antioxidant-rich, creamy goodness of this keto-friendly matcha smoothie.

These recipes offer a delightful array of beverages and smoothies to enhance your ketogenic journey, providing a balance of flavors and nutritional benefits to keep you energized and satisfied. Experiment with these recipes, adjusting ingredients to suit your taste preferences and dietary needs. Cheers to delicious and nourishing sips on your keto adventure!

# Chapter 9: Metabolic Nutrition and Cancer Care

In the realm of cancer treatment, metabolic nutrition has emerged as a promising complementary approach, offering potential benefits alongside traditional therapies. By understanding the intricate relationship between metabolism and cancer, we can harness the power of nutrition to influence tumor growth, enhance treatment efficacy, and improve overall patient outcomes.

## The Role of Metabolic Nutrition in Cancer Therapy

Cancer cells exhibit a distinct metabolic profile, characterized by an altered reliance on glucose fermentation for energy production, even in the presence of oxygen. This phenomenon, known as the Warburg effect, provides cancer cells with the resources they need to proliferate and resist apoptosis.

Metabolic nutrition aims to disrupt this metabolic imbalance by manipulating nutrient availability and metabolic processes. This can be achieved through various dietary interventions, such as:

- Ketogenic Diet: This low-carbohydrate, high-fat diet promotes the production of ketones, which can serve as an alternative energy source for normal cells while starving cancer cells.

- Intermittent Fasting: Periodic abstinence from food can trigger metabolic changes that may hinder cancer growth and enhance sensitivity to chemotherapy.

- Targeted Nutrient Therapies: Supplementation or restriction of specific nutrients can directly impact cancer cell metabolism.

# Understanding the Impact of Certain Foods on Cancer Growth

Certain dietary choices can influence cancer growth and treatment outcomes. For instance, high sugar intake has been linked to increased cancer risk and aggressiveness. Conversely, consumption of fruits, vegetables, and whole grains is associated with reduced cancer risk.

Specific foods have been shown to exert direct effects on cancer metabolism:

- Cruciferous Vegetables: Broccoli, cauliflower, and other cruciferous vegetables contain sulforaphane, a compound that can suppress cancer cell growth.

- Berries: Berry anthocyanins possess anti-inflammatory and antioxidant properties that may inhibit cancer progression.

- Green Tea: Green tea catechins exhibit anticancer effects by targeting cancer cell signaling pathways.

## Strategies for Combining Metabolic Nutrition with Chemotherapy

Metabolic nutrition can be effectively integrated with chemotherapy to potentially enhance treatment efficacy and reduce side effects:

- Nutrient Timing: Strategically scheduling nutrient intake around chemotherapy administration can minimize interference with the drugs' effects.

- Nutritional Supplementation: Addressing nutrient deficiencies and providing targeted nutritional support can improve tolerance to chemotherapy and overall well-being.

- Personalized Nutrition Plans: Tailoring dietary interventions to individual patient needs and cancer types can optimize treatment outcomes.

# Navigating Dietary Restrictions and Side Effects

Cancer patients often face dietary restrictions and side effects that can complicate nutrition management:

- Taste Alterations: Chemotherapy can alter taste perception, making it difficult to consume certain foods.

- Digestive Issues: Nausea, vomiting, and diarrhea can disrupt nutrient absorption and lead to malnutrition.

- Food Intolerances: Certain foods may trigger adverse reactions during cancer treatment.

**Effective strategies to address these challenges include:**

- Culinary Modifications: Adapting recipes and using flavor enhancers can improve palatability.

- Small, Frequent Meals: Eating smaller meals more often can reduce digestive discomfort.

- Individualized Dietary Plans: Working with a registered dietitian can ensure a personalized diet tailored to patient needs and treatment plan.

By incorporating metabolic nutrition into cancer care, we can empower patients to take an active role in their treatment and improve their overall health and well-being.

# Chapter 10: Embracing a Ketogenic Lifestyle

Adopting a ketogenic lifestyle involves more than just dietary changes. It encompasses a holistic approach to health and well-being, including incorporating regular exercise, managing stress, building a support system, and cultivating a positive mindset.

## Incorporating Exercise and Physical Activity into Your Keto Routine

Physical activity plays a crucial role in a ketogenic lifestyle, offering numerous benefits:

- Enhanced Weight Loss: Exercise promotes calorie burning and can accelerate weight loss when combined with a ketogenic diet.

- Improved Insulin Sensitivity: Regular physical activity enhances insulin sensitivity, which can aid in blood sugar control and overall metabolic health.

- Increased Muscle Mass: Exercise helps maintain muscle mass, which is essential for preserving metabolic rate and overall body composition.

- Boosted Energy Levels: Physical activity can elevate energy levels, counteracting fatigue sometimes associated with the ketogenic adaptation phase.

Aim for at least 30 minutes of moderate-intensity exercise most days of the week. Incorporate a variety of activities, such as brisk walking, jogging, cycling, swimming, or strength training.

Strength training exercise for ketogenic lifestyle

# Managing Stress and Emotional Eating While on Keto

Stress can trigger emotional eating, which can undermine the success of a ketogenic diet. Here are some strategies to manage stress and emotional eating:

- Identify Stressors: Recognize the situations or triggers that induce stress and develop coping mechanisms.

- Practice Relaxation Techniques: Engage in activities like meditation, yoga, or deep breathing to promote relaxation and reduce stress levels.

- Seek Support: Talk to a therapist or counselor if stress is overwhelming and interfering with your ketogenic journey.

- Plan Meals Ahead: Prepare meals in advance to avoid making impulsive food choices when stressed.

- Indulge in Healthy Alternatives: When cravings strike, opt for keto-friendly snacks like nuts, seeds, or low-sugar dark chocolate.

## Building a Support System for Long-Term Keto Success

Surrounding yourself with a supportive network can significantly enhance your ketogenic journey:

- Find a Ketogenic Community: Join online forums, local support groups, or connect with friends and family who are also on keto.

- Partner with an Accountability Buddy: Having a support partner can provide encouragement, motivation, and accountability.

- Seek Professional Guidance: Consult a registered dietitian or nutritionist specializing in ketogenic diets for personalized advice and support.

- Attend Ketogenic Seminars or Workshops: Participate in educational events to gain knowledge and interact with other keto enthusiasts.

- Utilize Online Resources: Explore websites, blogs, and social media groups dedicated to ketogenic living for inspiration and information.

## Ketogenic support group

Maintaining a Positive Mindset and Embracing a Healthy Lifestyle

Embracing a ketogenic lifestyle requires a positive mindset and a commitment to overall well-being:

- Set Realistic Goals: Establish achievable goals and celebrate your progress along the way.

- Focus on Long-Term Health: View keto as a sustainable lifestyle choice rather than a quick fix.

- Practice Self-Compassion: Be kind to yourself and avoid self-criticism when facing setbacks.

- Prioritize Sleep: Aim for 7-8 hours of quality sleep each night to support metabolic function and overall health.

- Manage Expectations: Understand that weight loss and metabolic changes may vary from person to person.

- Embrace a Holistic Approach: View keto as part of a broader lifestyle that includes physical activity, stress management, and mental well-being.

By incorporating these strategies into your ketogenic journey, you can set yourself up for long-term success and achieve your health and wellness goals. Remember, embracing a ketogenic lifestyle is about more than just restricting carbohydrates; it's about adopting a holistic approach to health and well-being that nourishes your body, mind, and spirit.

# Conclusion

The ketogenic diet has emerged as a powerful tool in the fight against cancer, offering potential benefits in cancer prevention, treatment, and recovery. By understanding the intricate relationship between metabolism and cancer, we can harness the power of nutrition to disrupt cancer cell growth and enhance treatment efficacy.

## Empowering Yourself with Knowledge and Dietary Choices

In the face of a cancer diagnosis, the ability to make informed dietary choices can be a source of empowerment and control. By delving into the science behind the ketogenic diet, individuals can make conscious decisions about their food intake, potentially influencing their treatment outcomes and overall well-being.

## Embracing a Holistic Approach to Cancer Care and Overall Well-being

While the ketogenic diet holds promise in the realm of cancer care, it is essential to recognize that it is one piece of a comprehensive treatment plan. A holistic approach to cancer care encompasses traditional therapies, nutritional interventions, physical activity, stress management, and emotional support.

## Resources for Further Exploration and Support

Numerous resources are available to guide individuals on their ketogenic journey and provide support during cancer treatment:

- Websites: Charlie Foundation, Ketogenic Science, Defeat Cancer with Keto, and Cancer Research UK

- Online Communities: Keto for Cancer Facebook Group, Cancer Ketogenic Diet Support Group, and Keto for Cancer Warriors Forum

- Registered Dietitians (RDs): Consult an RD specializing in cancer nutrition for personalized guidance and support.

As you navigate the complexities of cancer treatment, remember that you are not alone. Embrace the power of knowledge, seek support from loved ones and professionals, and approach your ketogenic journey with a positive mindset and a determination to reclaim your health and well-being.

Made in the USA
Las Vegas, NV
18 February 2024